AR BL 4.6
0.5 pt.
X

The LIFE CYCLE of an EARTHWORM

Andrew Hipp

Photographs by Dwight Kuhn

The Rosen Publishing Group's
PowerKids Press™
New York

For many evening walks at the Arboretum, listening to the worms—Andrew Hipp
For Stephen—Dwight Kuhn

Published in 2002 by The Rosen Publishing Group, Inc.
29 East 21st Street, New York, NY 10010

First Edition

Book Design: Michael Caroleo and Michael de Guzman

Project Editor: Emily Raabe

Photo Credits: All photos © Dwight Kuhn

Hipp, Andrew.
The life cycle of an earthworm / Andrew Hipp.
     p. cm. — (The life cycles library)
Includes bibliographical references (p.   ).
ISBN 0-8239-5870-1 (lib. bdg.)
1. Earthworms—Life cycles—Juvenile literature. [1. Earthworms.] I. Title.
QL391.A6 H57 2002
592'.64—dc21
                                                        2001000144

Manufactured in the United States of America

What Is an Earthworm?

Earthworms are among the strangest of all animals that live in the soil. They have no eyes or ears. They have no bones. They don't even have lungs! Earthworms have several hearts. Their long brown or red bodies are filled with a slimy liquid that they use to keep their skin moist. Earthworms sometimes **secrete** this liquid, covering their skin with it. The liquid tastes bad to **predators** who might like to eat earthworms.

◀ *Earthworms breathe through their skin. If an earthworm dries out, it will not be able to breathe.*

Mating

Earthworms are **hermaphrodites**, which means that each worm is both male and female. Some kinds of earthworms are able to make babies all by themselves. Most of them, however, need other earthworms to mate. Two worms lie belly to belly on the soil's surface or beneath the soil. They grasp each other using tiny hairs, called **setae**. Then each worm squirts out a tiny amount of **sperm**, which the other worm stores inside its body.

Worms mate for as long as an hour before leaving each other to make cocoons. The small picture shows an earthworm's setae. ▶

Cocoons

After mating, each earthworm makes a cocoon around the middle of its body. The cocoon fits snugly around the worm like a tiny rubber band. The earthworm fills it with eggs and sperm. The earthworm also puts food for its babies into the cocoon. Then the earthworm wriggles backward, sliding the cocoon up and over its head. The ends of the cocoon close up and the earthworm leaves it in the soil. The earthworm continues to make cocoons until its stored sperm is used up.

◀ *These earthworm cocoons are each no bigger than a grain of rice. Cocoons may take from two weeks to four months to hatch.*

Hatching and Growing

Newly hatched worms are colorless, and they cannot mate. Young worms may take anywhere from a few months to a year to become old enough to mate. If a worm is cut in half, it probably will die. However, if a worm's head or tail is cut off, it may regrow the parts that have been cut off. This process is called **regeneration**. Not all species of earthworms can do this. The rear end of a worm grows back more quickly than the front end does.

Because earthworms are born colorless, you can see the inside of this hatching earthworm's body. ▶

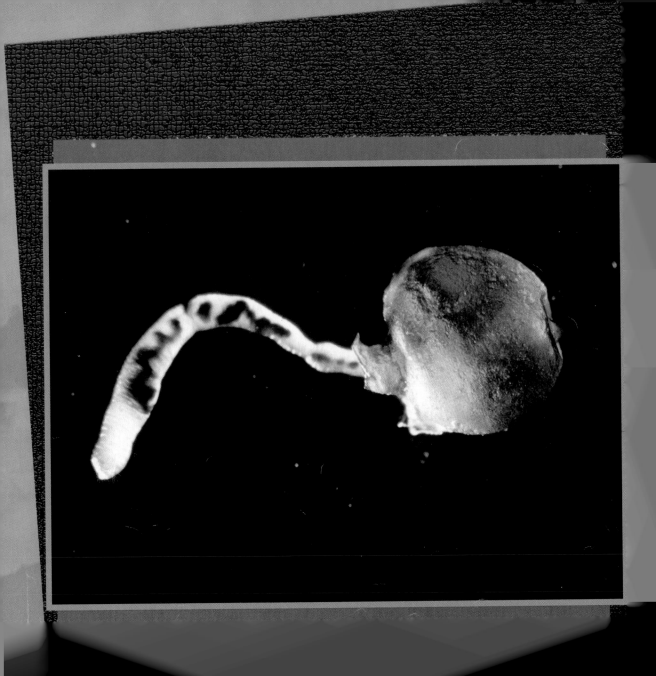

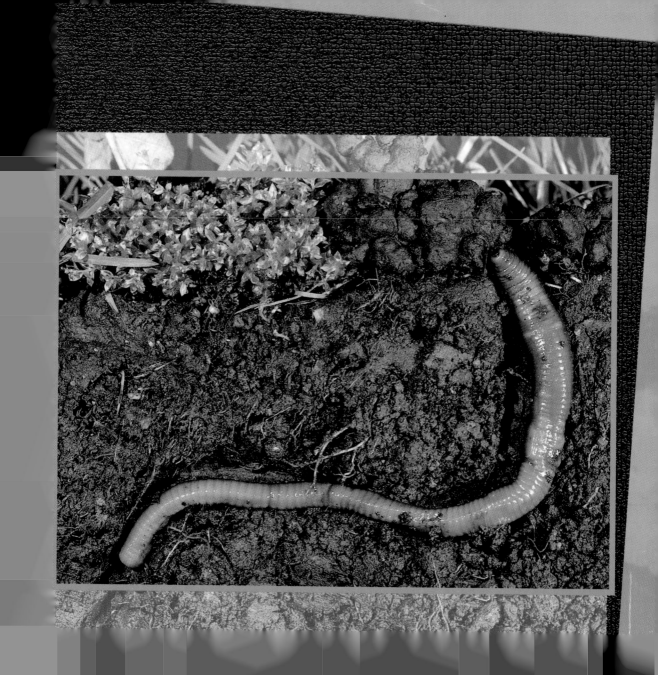

Crawling

Earthworms get around very well without hands and feet. Using their setae, worms hold onto the soil and pull their back ends forward to move. Although worms can't see or hear, chemicals in the soil help worms sense food and other worms that might become mates. Worms sense light using sensors near their heads and tails. They also feel **vibrations**. If you put a heavy stick in the ground and pound it with a mallet, the vibrations in the soil may bring worms to the surface.

◄ *Worms wiggle if you hold them in your hand. They like to have all surfaces of their body touched at the same time. In this photo, dirt surrounds an earthworm in its burrow.*

Making Burrows

Many kinds of earthworms dig tunnels through the ground. These tunnels are called burrows. Burrows may be 6 feet (2 m) deep. Worms will mate, eat, and **hibernate** in their burrows. If the topsoil becomes hot or dry, worms will go deep into their burrows to stay cool and moist. Burrows help keep the soil moist and full of oxygen. This helps plants' roots to get the air and water they need to grow. Without worms, plants would have a hard time living.

Worms are great friends to gardeners. Some kinds, though, like nightcrawlers, are so large that they can ▶ tear garden plants right out of the ground!

Eating

Earthworms eat fallen leaves, dead plant roots, animal parts, and soil. Food and soil that they suck in through their mouths is stored in little sacs called **crops**. From there, the food passes into their **gizzards**, which are filled with bits of stone and sand. The gizzards grind the food. The food then passes through long, straight **intestines**. The intestines absorb **nutrients** from the food. What is left after the nutrients have been absorbed passes from the worms as **castings**.

This earthworm is pulling a leaf down into the ground to eat later. Worms eat leaves and turn them into rich soil.

Castings

As earthworms grind up and **digest** their food, they mix it with **bacteria**. These bacteria continue to break down the food even after it leaves a worm's body in piles of casts. These casts provide nutrients for the plants growing nearby. Casts look like little piles of soil. In fact, earthworm casts are soil, and they are safe to touch. Piles of casts are usually about as big as a walnut shell. Some kinds of earthworms, however, can make towers of castings 3 inches (7.5 cm) tall.

Nightcrawlers' casts are often found right near the entrance to a burrow. They are lumpy and soft to the touch, like rich soil. ▶

Making Soil

Earthworms may eat from 2 to 30 times their own weight in food and soil each day. As they tunnel through the soil, eating and making casts, they turn dead plant parts into soil. In this way, leaves, fruits, and roots become plant food. As pets, earthworms may live from four to ten years. In the wild, they often live for only a year. They may die from lack of water, or get eaten by a mole, mouse, bird, or other predator. After they die, earthworms themselves turn into soil.

◀ *After these earthworms die, they will rot into the soil. This soil will provide food for plants, which will provide food for more worms.*

Earthworm Invaders

Big sheets of ice, called glaciers, covered North America for much of the past 2.5 million years. When the glaciers melted, they left the ground bare. There were no plants or earthworms. Plants soon returned, but the earthworms took a long time to come back. Some parts of Canada still have no earthworms! Today there are more than 30 kinds of earthworms in the United States. If you go outside at night with an adult, listen closely. You might hear earthworms moving in the leaves, pulling food down into their burrows.

Glossary

bacteria (bak-TEER-ee-uh) A group of microscopic living things.

castings (KAST-ingz) A worm's waste products, also called casts.

crops (KROPS) Stomach-like sacs in which food is stored for digestion.

digest (dy-JEST) To break down the food one has eaten in order to get nutrients out of it.

gizzards (GIH-zurdz) Grit-filled sacs in which birds, worms, and some other animals grind their food.

hermaphrodites (her-MA-froh-dyts) Animals that have both male and female mating parts.

hibernate (HY-bur-nayt) To spend the winter in a state of rest.

intestines (in-TES-tinz) The long tubes inside animals' bodies that absorb nutrients from food after the food has been eaten.

nutrients (NOO-tree-ints) The substances in food or soil that support life.

predators (PREH-duh-terz) Animals that kill other animals for food.

regeneration (ri-jeh-nuh-RAY-shun) Producing something again.

secrete (sih-KREET) To make and give off from the body.

setae (SEH-tee) The hairs on a worm's body.

sperm (SPERM) Fluid that male animals produce when mating.

vibrations (vy-BRAY-shunz) Rapid, back and forth movements.

Index

Web Sites

To learn more about earthworms, check out these Web sites:

www.nysite.com/nature/fauna/earthworm.htm

www.urbanext.uiuc.edu/worms/